MAR - - 2017

MIGHTY MACHINES IN ACTION

Police Cars

by Emily Rose Oachs

BELLWETHER MEDIA • MINNEAPOLIS, MN

Note to Librarians, Teachers, and Parents:

Blastoff! Readers are carefully developed by literacy experts and combine standards-based content with developmentally appropriate text.

Level 1 provides the most support through repetition of high-frequency words, light text, predictable sentence patterns, and strong visual support.

Level 2 offers early readers a bit more challenge through varied simple sentences, increased text load, and less repetition of high-frequency words.

Level 3 advances early-fluent readers toward fluency through increased text and concept load, less reliance on visuals, longer sentences, and more literary language.

Level 4 builds reading stamina by providing more text per page, increased use of punctuation, greater variation in sentence patterns, and increasingly challenging vocabulary.

Level 5 encourages children to move from "learning to read" to "reading to learn" by providing even more text, varied writing styles, and less familiar topics.

Whichever book is right for your reader, Blastoff! Readers are the perfect books to build confidence and encourage a love of reading that will last a lifetime!

This edition first published in 2017 by Bellwether Media, Inc.

No part of this publication may be reproduced in whole or in part without written permission of the publisher. For information regarding permission, write to Bellwether Media, Inc., Attention: Permissions Department, 5357 Penn Avenue South, Minneapolis, MN 55419.

Library of Congress Cataloging-in-Publication Data

Names: Oachs, Emily Rose, author.
Title: Police Cars / by Emily Rose Oachs.
Description: Minneapolis, MN : Bellwether Media, Inc., 2017. | Series:
   Blastoff! Readers. Mighty Machines in Action | Audience: Ages 5-8. |
   Audience: K to grade 3. | Includes bibliographical references and index.
Identifiers: LCCN 2016034509 (print) | LCCN 2016037681 (ebook) | ISBN
   9781626176072 (hardcover : alk. paper) | ISBN 9781681033372 (ebook)
Subjects: LCSH: Police vehicles–Juvenile literature. | Police–Equipment and
   supplies–Juvenile literature.
Classification: LCC HV7936.V4 O23 2017 (print) | LCC HV7936.V4 (ebook) | DDC
   363.2/32–dc23
LC record available at https://lccn.loc.gov/2016034509

Editor: Christina Leighton   Designer: Jon Eppard

Printed in the United States of America, North Mankato, MN.

Table of **Contents**

BRINGING HELP

A police car **cruises** down a city street. Then its lights start to flash and its **siren** sounds.

Wee-ooo! It zooms
past other cars.

The police car stops near a car crash. A police officer rushes out.

Thanks to the police car, the officer is there to help!

CARS ON PATROL

Police cars help police officers **patrol** roads, cities, and towns.

8

They go where their work calls them!

COMMON POLICE CARS

Ford Crown Victoria

Chevy Impala

Dodge Charger

Most police cars are **sedans** or **sport utility vehicles** (SUVs).

sport utility
vehicle

sedan

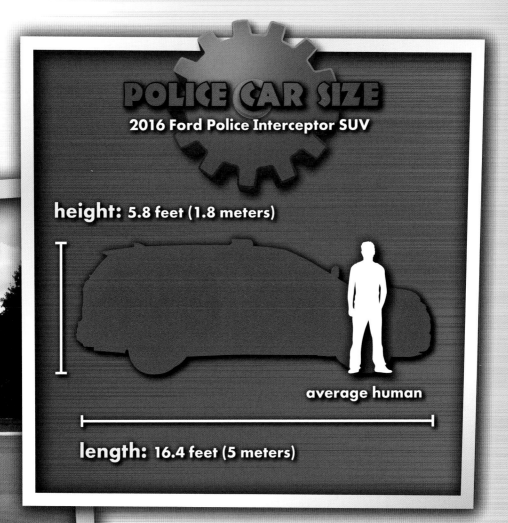

POLICE CAR SIZE

2016 Ford Police Interceptor SUV

height: 5.8 feet (1.8 meters)

average human

length: 16.4 feet (5 meters)

SUVs are becoming more popular. They carry a lot of gear.

98

FARGO P

Sworn to Protect • De

logo

Police cars are painted to stand out from other cars. Many are black and white.

On the sides are **logos** of the police force.

A light bar sits
on each police
car's roof.

light bar

It flashes red and blue lights.
The lights help let people know
the car's location.

Inside, officers talk on a **two-way radio**.

two-way
radio

IDENTIFY A POLICE CAR

light bar

cage

NYPD Courtesy Professionalism Respect

logo

A cage and **bulletproof** glass separate the front and back seats. They help protect police officers.

Police cars rush
to **emergencies**.

Some reach speeds up to 150 miles (241 kilometers) per hour!

A police car's lights and loud siren send a message. Watch out! The police car is on the move.

Wherever they go, police cars help keep communities safe.

Glossary

bulletproof—unable to break from the force of bullets

cruises—drives steadily

emergencies—serious and dangerous events that need quick attention

logos—symbols or designs that label something

patrol—to go through an area to make sure it is safe

sedans—cars with four doors and a top that usually cannot be removed

siren—an instrument that makes warning sounds

sport utility vehicles—large automobiles with extra storage space that can be driven on rough ground; sport utility vehicles are also called SUVs.

two-way radio—a radio that lets people talk and listen to each other

To Learn More

AT THE LIBRARY

Morey, Allan. *Police Cars*. Minneapolis, Minn.: Bullfrog Books, 2015.

Olien, Becky. *Police Cars in Action*. Mankato, Minn.: Capstone Press, 2012.

Spaight, Anne J. *Police Cars on the Go*. Minneapolis, Minn.: Lerner Publications, 2017.

ON THE WEB

Learning more about police cars is as easy as 1, 2, 3.

1. Go to www.factsurfer.com.

2. Enter "police cars" into the search box.

3. Click the "Surf" button and you will see a list of related web sites.

With factsurfer.com, finding more information is just a click away.

Index

The images in this book are reproduced through the courtesy of: FCA US LLC, front cover, pp. 18, 18-19, 20-21; The Ford Motor Company/ FCA, pp. 4-5, 5, 6-7, 10-11, 14; Matthew Richardson/ Alamy, p. 8; Philip Lange, p. 9 (top); Leonard Zhukovsky, pp. 9 (center, bottom), 17 (bottom); csfotoimages, pp. 12-13; TFoxFoto, p. 15; Avid Creative, Inc., p. 16; kandypix, p. 17 (top left); Amy Johansson, p. 17 (top right); Dwight Smith, p. 20.